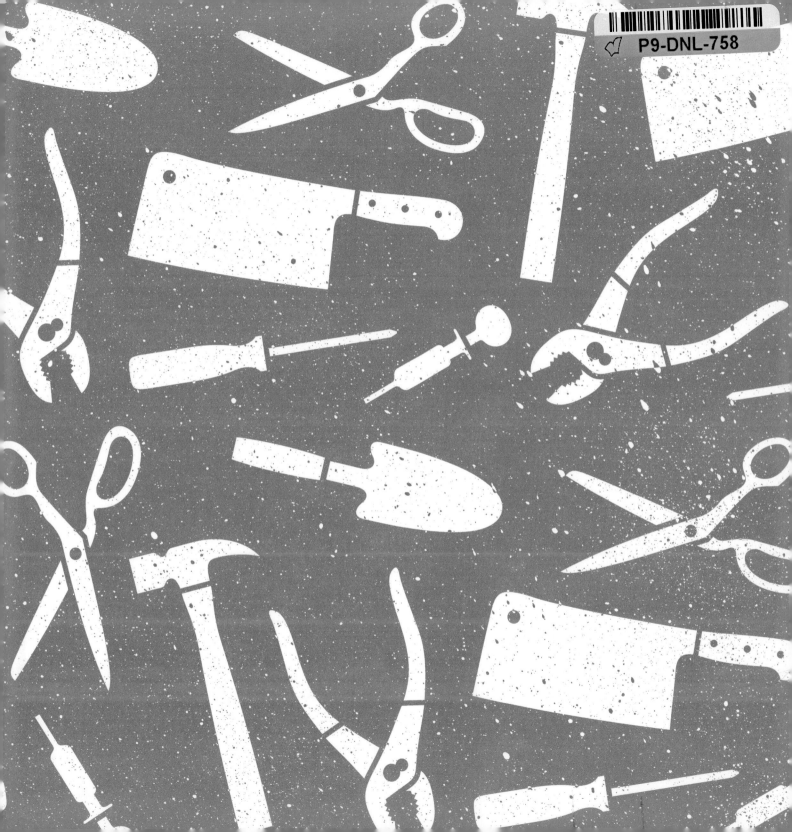

P9-DNL-758

First published in the United States in 2006 by Chronicle Books LLC.

Copyright © 2005 by Taro Miura.
Originally published in Italy in 2005 by Maurizio Corraini srl.

Book design by corrainiStudio.
Typeset in Bodoni Egyptian, Cooper Black, Helvetica, Hermes Black,
ITC Bookman, ITC Kabel, ITC Lubalin Graph, Linoscript, Neutraface
Display, OCRA, Times and Futura BT.
The illustrations in this book were rendered in Adobe Illustrator
and Adobe Photoshop.
Manufactured in Italy.

Library of Congress Cataloging-in-Publication Data
Miura, Taro, 1955-
  Tools / by Taro Miura.
     p. cm.
  ISBN-13: 978-0-8118-5519-8
  ISBN-10: 0-8118-5519-8
  1. Tools—Juvenile literature. I. Title.
  TJ1195.M58 2006
  621.9—dc22
2005034057

Distributed in Canada by Raincoast Books
9050 Shaughnessy Street, Vancouver, British Columbia V6P 6E5

10 9 8 7 6 5 4 3 2 1

Chronicle Books LLC
85 Second Street, San Francisco, California 94105

www.chroniclekids.com

TARO MIURA

TOOLS

chronicle books · san francisco

hammer

clamp

try square

saw

nails

chisel

Carpenter

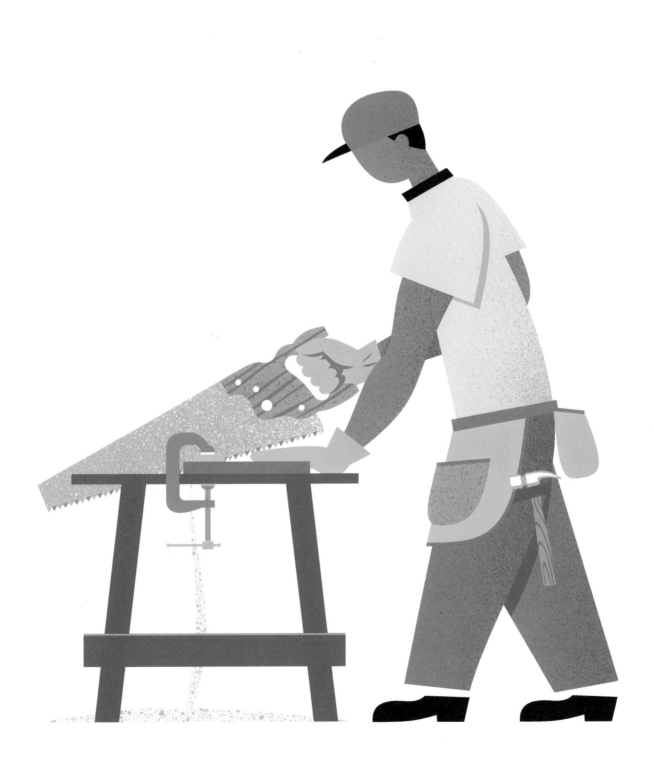

pins

pincushion

thread

measuring tape

21 20 19 18 17 16 15 14 13 12 11 10 9 8 7 6

scissors

chalk

pinking shears

5 4 3 2 1

Tailor

adjustable
wrench

slotted
screwdriver

open-end
wrench

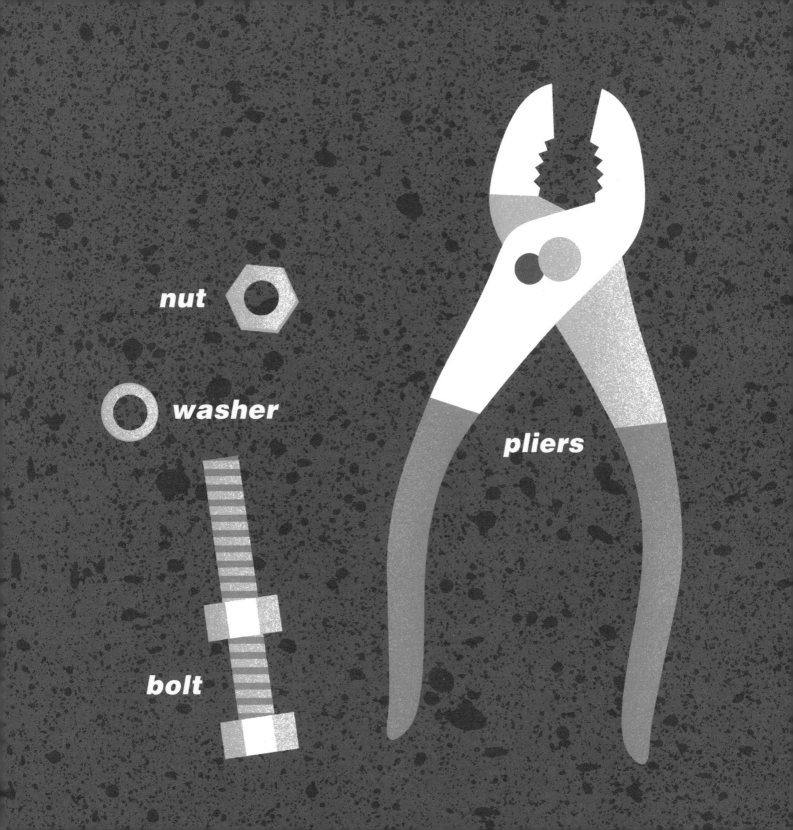

nut

washer

bolt

pliers

Mechanic

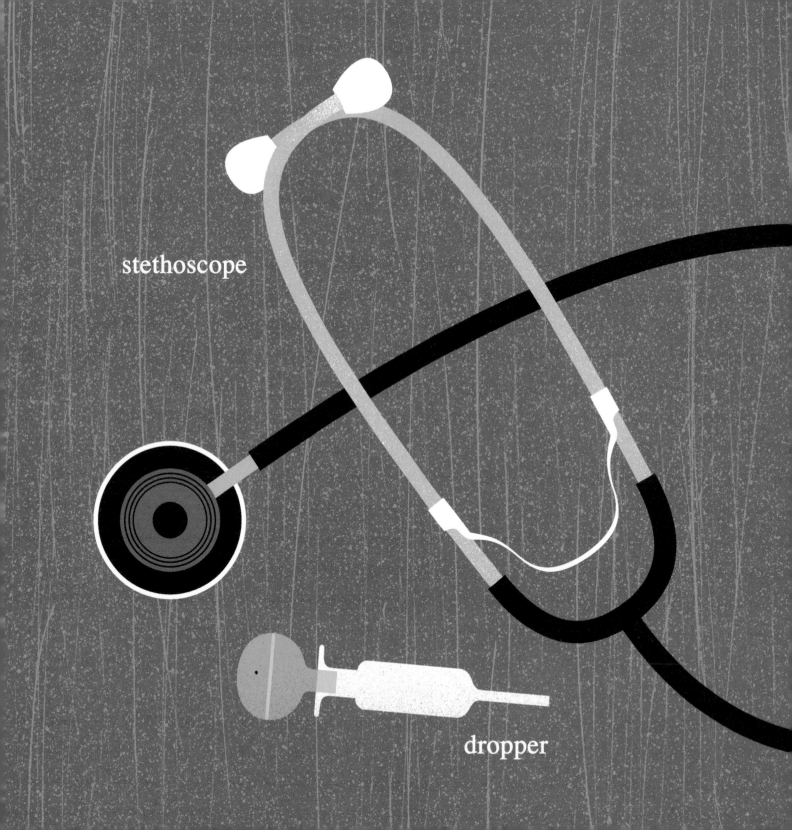

stethoscope

dropper

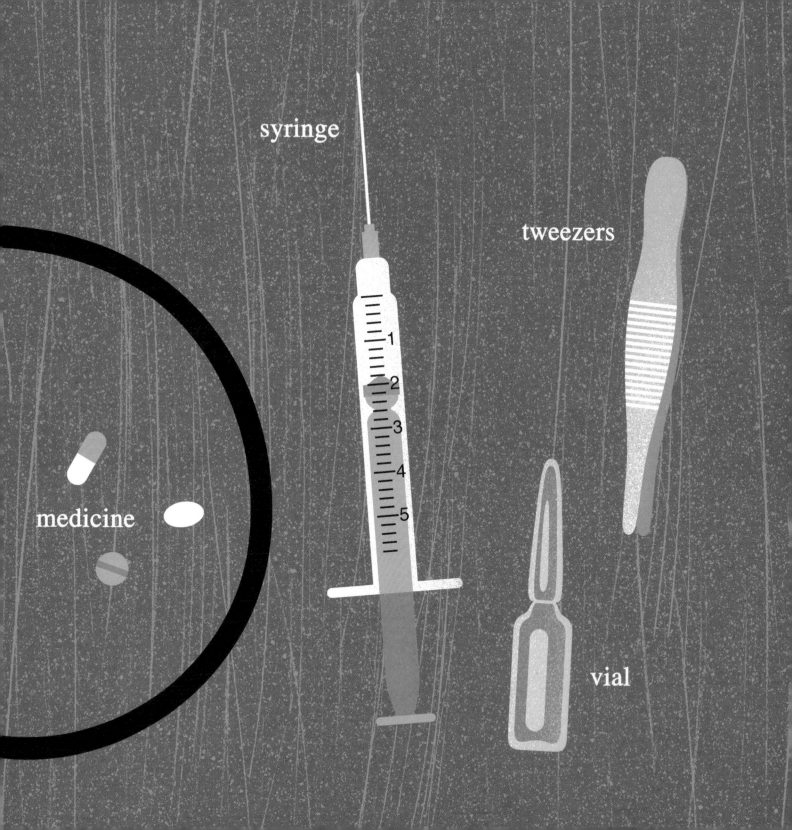

syringe

tweezers

medicine

vial

1
2
3
4
5

Doctor

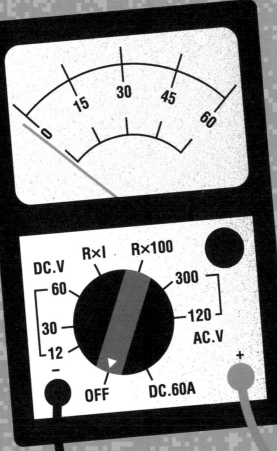

voltage
tester

DC.V
R×I R×100
60
300
30
120
12
AC.V
−
OFF DC.60A
+

15 30 45 60
0

screw

Phillips-head
screwdriver

soldering
wire

needle-nose
pliers

soldering
iron

Electrician

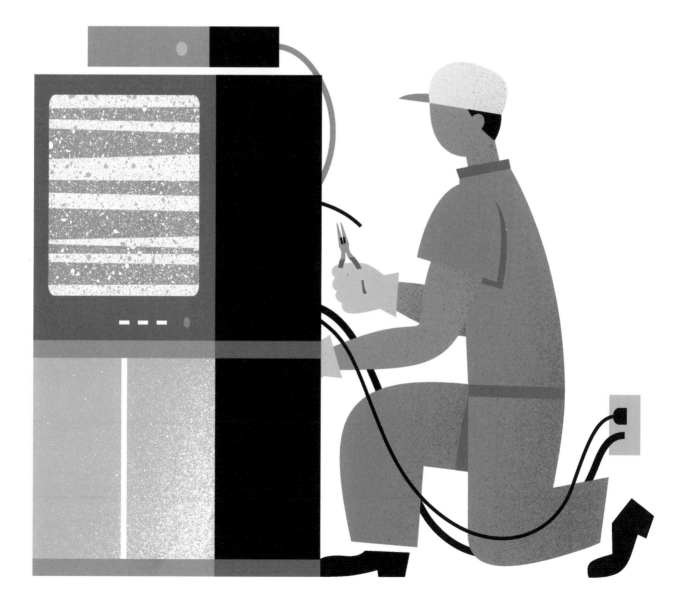

hedge shears

shovel

gardening fork

trowel

watering can

Gardener

knife

measuring cup

200
150
100
50

spatula

cleaver

measuring
spoons

pot

Chef

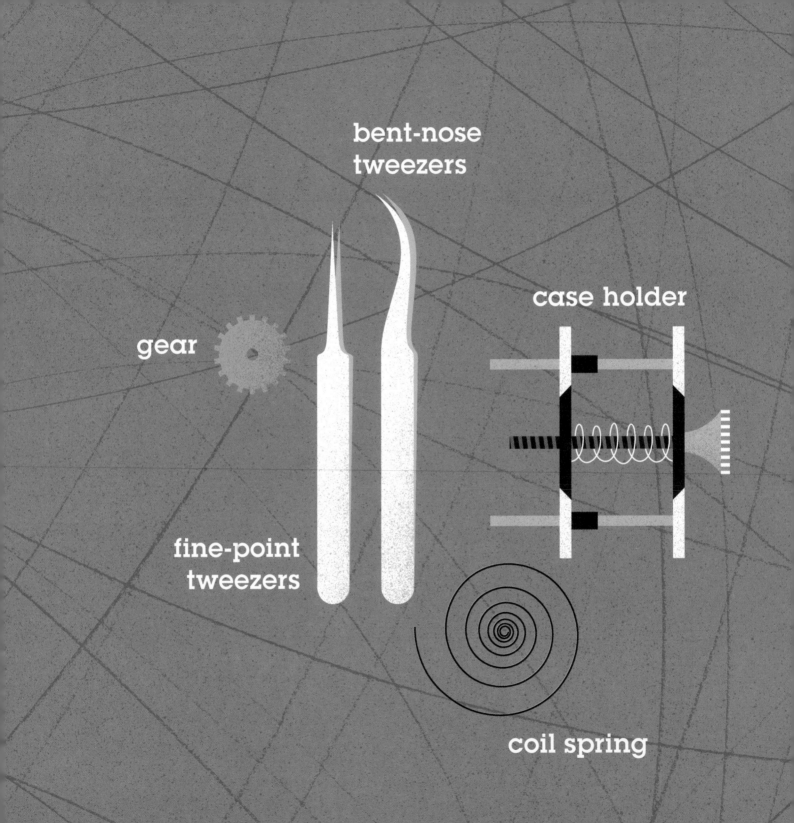

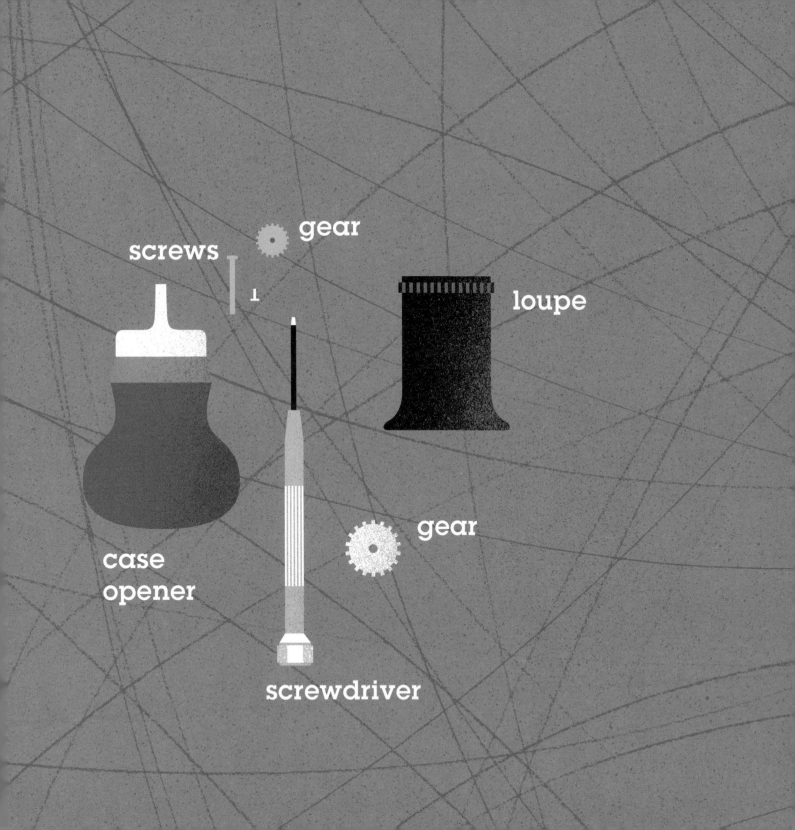

screws

gear

loupe

case opener

gear

screwdriver

Watchmaker

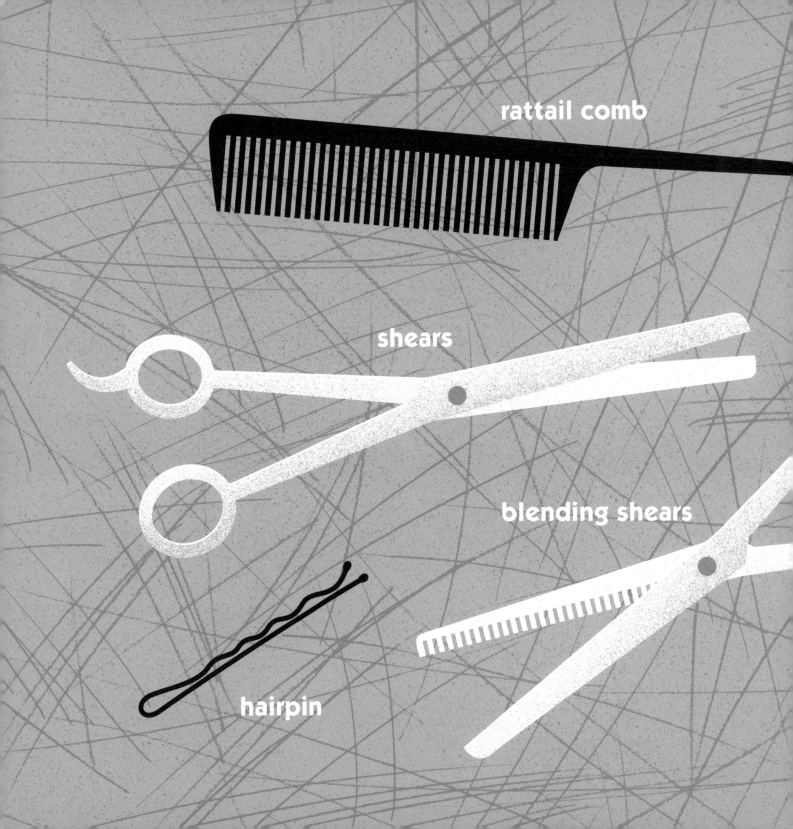

rattail comb

shears

blending shears

hairpin

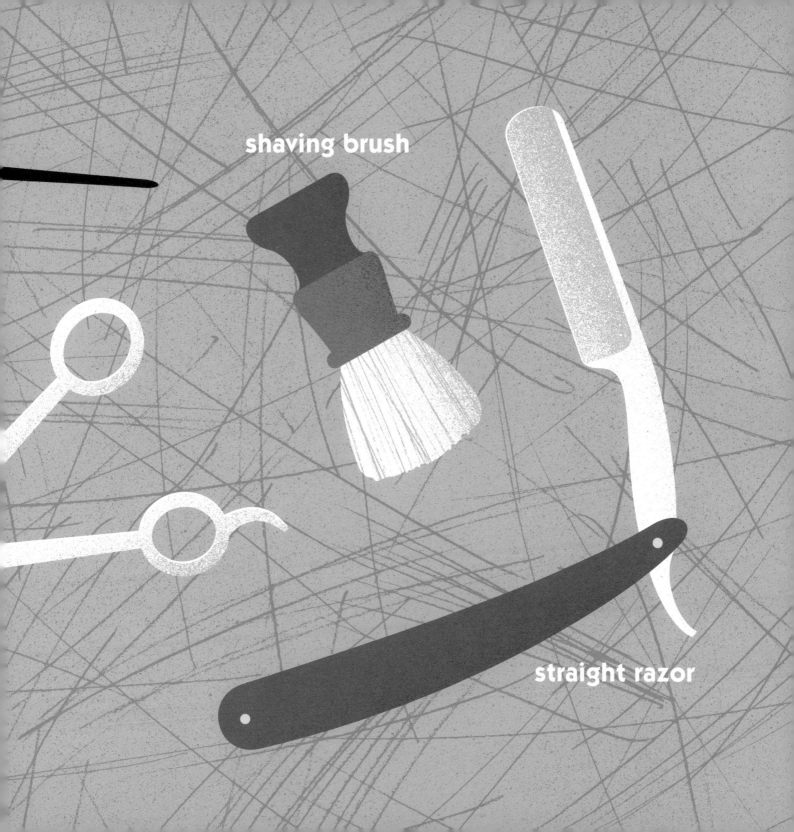

shaving brush

straight razor

Barber

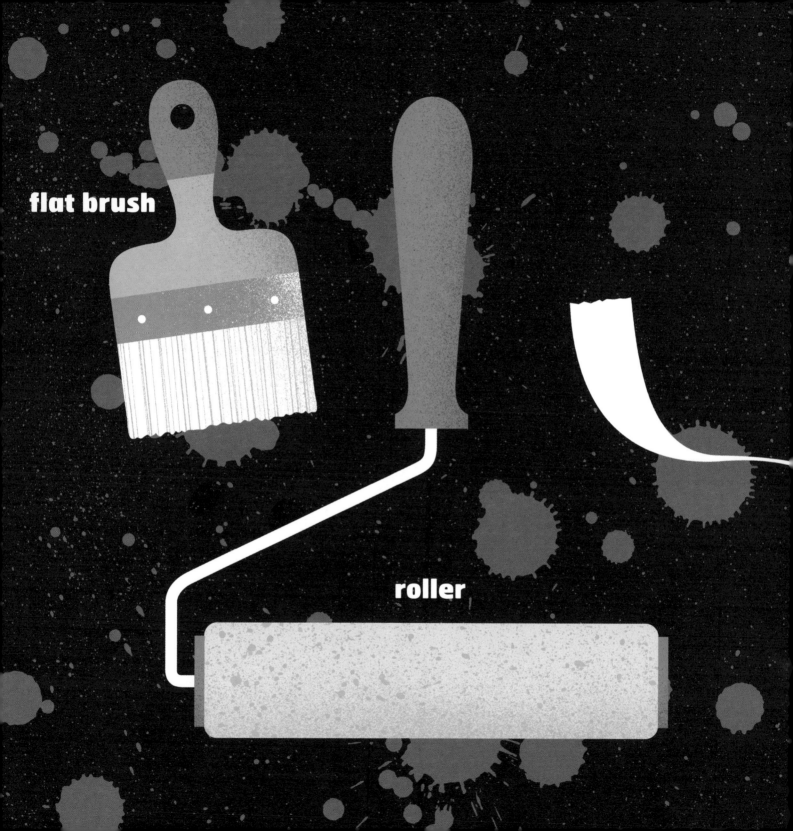

flat brush

roller

angled brush

paint thinner

masking tape

Painter